JEREMY H.

MEDIEVAL POTTERY
IN BRITAIN

2

Cover illustration
Fourteenth-century jug of off-white or buff sandy fabric
with impressed wheat-ear decoration; probably made in Surrey.
(Museum of London)

Published by
SHIRE PUBLICATIONS LTD
Cromwell House, Church Street, Princes Risborough,
Aylesbury, Bucks, HP17 9AJ, U.K.

Series Editor: James Dyer

ISBN 0 7478 0010 3

First published 1978
Second edition 1984, reprinted 1989

Printed in Great Britain by
C. I. Thomas & Sons (Haverfordwest) Ltd
Press Buildings, Merlins Bridge, Haverfordwest.

Contents

List of illustrations

Preface

The text of this book is essentially complementary to the series of drawings of pottery vessels in figures 1-29. In these I have tried to illustrate the diversity of types produced in Great Britain between AD 850 and 1500, rather than to set out formal type series. I have also had to be highly selective. Much excavated pottery has not yet been published; of the material which has, more has had to be omitted than has been included.

The drawings

The illustrated vessels are referred to in the text by the figure and drawing number (e.g. **16**, 8). All the drawings are reproduced at one-eighth scale, except for **2**, 1 and 2, which are at one-tenth scale.

The drawings are in most cases taken from published examples, and these are credited to the author of the article in which they appear. Pottery vessels drawn by the writer are credited 'author'; most of these, in particular those from London, have not been published before. Reconstructions are incorporated in some of the drawings, but where otherwise published are not shown as such; only my own reconstructions of incomplete vessels are shown as broken lines. Different coloured slips used as painted or trailed decoration are shown as solid black (red slip) or dotted (white slip). In common with standard archaeological practice, all the drawings have been shaded as though the light is coming from the top left-hand corner of the page.

Acknowledgements

I must thank all those who have allowed me to use their published material; acknowledgement is given in the captions to the drawings. R. C. Alvey (Nottingham University) has also kindly allowed me to use some of his own unpublished drawings. Thanks must also go to the curators and staff of the following museums, who have helped me in my study of material in their care, and who have allowed the use of my own drawings of it in this book: Ashmolean Museum, Oxford; Bank of England Museum, London; Bristol City Museum; British Museum; Kingston-upon-Thames Museum; Museum of London; Maidstone Museum;

Victoria and Albert Museum, London; Fitzwilliam Museum Cambridge; and Winchester City Museum.

I must also express my gratitude to the West Surrey College of Art and Design (Farnham), which by giving me a Research Fellowship in the history of ceramics in the period 1971-4 allowed most of the work on the London material to be undertaken.

My wife, Claudia, has also been of unfailing help throughout all stages of the production of both text and drawings.

Preface to the second edition

Several changes have been made in the text of this book, in particular to the sections on Oxford and London, where recent work has added considerably to our knowledge of the types in use, their date and distribution and, in many cases, their source of production. I am grateful to Maureen Mellor and to Jackie Pearce and Alan Vince for new information on the pottery from Oxford and London respectively. Recent work has in general tended to suggest an earlier date for many types of pottery in both the pre- and post-conquest periods.

The illustrations have not been changed, even though much new material has appeared in print (see the section Further Reading). There are some areas, the south-east, east and north of England in particular, where more material is now available than can be included in the space available in this book. It must be emphasised therefore that the drawings are not intended to be representative of the range of types present on particular places or areas, but merely illustrations of a selection of them.

Glossary and techniques

Anthropomorphic and zoomorphic decoration: Semi-abstract decoration of human or animal motifs executed with *applied* or *trailed slip* and commonest on jugs of the thirteenth and fourteenth centuries. Human motifs include figures outlined in trailed slip (**23,** 16; **25,** 8); faces, usually with beards, on the necks of jugs, sometimes forming their spouts, and arms with hands holding the chin (**17,** 2-4; **21,** 12; **22,** 11-12; **26,** 8 and 10-11); or mounted knights in high relief (**28,** 11). Zoomorphic decoration consists of stags or hunting scenes (**13,** 10; **15,** 7); or heraldic beasts (**16,** 7), some of them copying French prototypes.

Biscuit firing: The technique of firing vessels twice, the first time without and the second time with the glaze. Used widely in pottery-making in medieval France and introduced into England with green-glazed *Tudor green ware* in the late fifteenth century.

Carination: A sharp change of angle in the profile of some jugs (**13,** 1-4; **19,** 10-13).

Fabric: The constituents and appearance of the clay of the fired vessel.

Glaze: The transparent, sometimes coloured, vitrified covering of much medieval pottery after *c.* 1100, though in use on some types (e.g. Stamford-type wares and Winchester ware) from much earlier. The use of lead sulphide or oxide gives a yellow glaze; powdered galena (lead sulphide) was used in the Midlands (e.g. splashed glaze ware in Nottingham) in the early medieval period. Glaze was commonly coloured green by the addition of copper compounds, from the twelfth century at Stamford, and from the thirteenth century elsewhere.

Oxidation and reduction: Firing conditions in a kiln can be controlled so that the pottery bakes in an atmosphere either rich or deficient in oxygen. The latter state, leading to reduction, turns the pottery grey or black, owing to the formation of green ferrous oxide (FeO) from the free iron in the clay. Oxidation turns the pottery brown, buff or off-white, according to the proportion of iron in the clay, owing to the formation of rust-coloured ferric oxide (Fe_2O_3).

Rouletting: The technique of decorating the body or rim of the pot with a wheel carved with geometric patterns. Its use is commonest in the earlier periods (e.g. **2,** 4; **3,** 13 and 18; **5,** 12-13; **8,** 3-4 and 10), following continental practices, but it is also found on some thirteenth-century jugs from Yorkshire (**28,** 5, 7 and 9).

Sagging or convex bases: One of the distinctive features of all types of
early medieval pottery. It has been stated that this feature was in part
accidental, the result of dragging the finished pot from the wheel.
Anyone who has made a pot will know that this is not so. Bases of this
kind are made quite deliberately, usually by careful shaping with a
knife after the removal of the vessel from the wheel, or less usually by
the luting of a shaped slab of clay to the bottom of a turned pot. There
is evidence from excavated examples for the use of both techniques in
the medieval period. Their purpose was to prevent the pot cracking
during periods of thermal instability, both in the firing and in the use of
the vessel on a fire. The term 'convex base' indicates this deliberate
technique rather better than the term 'sagging base', though the latter
has become established in the literature.

Slip, paint: A suspension of fine clay in water, used either to cover the
exterior of a vessel by dipping or painting (usually with white slip on a
vessel with red fabric), or as a means of decoration. This took several
forms: *trailed slip* — formed by squeezing out continuous lines from a
horn or pouch, as a cake is decorated with icing (**12**, 3; **13**, 1-3; **16**, 1-6);
painted slip — put on with a brush or rag (**12**, 7-8; **14**, 7-10; **15**, 11-14);
applied slip — the use of a stiffer mix to decorate the pot with pads,
lines, scales or anthropomorphic or zoomorphic motifs. Iron-rich or
iron-free clay can be used to give a red or a white colour after firing.

Tempering or gritting: The agents added to the clay to give stability in
both throwing and firing. In the early medieval period this was usually
crushed shell, requiring a low firing temperature (under 850C). The
increasing use of quartz sand instead of shell through the medieval
period (but used at an early date in Thetford-type ware) enabled higher
firing temperatures to be achieved.

Wheel-throwing: Most pottery is shaped or thrown on a horizontal wheel.
This is described by archaeologists (though not by potters) as either a
fast or a *slow wheel*. The latter is a form of turntable which has to be
rotated with one hand while the pot is formed with the other. A *fast
wheel* is one with an independent means of motion given by a flywheel
which is turned either by the feet or by a stick, and which allows the pot
to be formed with both hands. *Hand-made* pottery is built up from coils
or slabs, without the use of a wheel, though finishing is often carried
out on a turntable. If more attention were paid by medieval archaeologists to ethnographic parallels much of the confusion inherent
in the use of these terms could be avoided.

1
Introduction

Pottery is often found in large quantities during the archaeological excavation of medieval sites; it is sometimes therefore regarded merely as a useful dating tool, to be analysed, written up and then forgotten. Yet this approach ignores its most important aspect, common perhaps to pottery of all periods: that being cheaply and easily made, frequently broken and discarded, and being virtually indestructible once buried, its excavated remains reflect more closely than do those of any other type of artefact the social, economic and cultural changes within society.

It can, perhaps most importantly, provide evidence for the history and development of manufacturing processes and the transmission of specific skills. In the six centuries covered in this book pottery-making in England developed from a primitive village craft (if it existed at all) to a highly sophisticated and in places large-scale industry. In most cases the only evidence for these changes is the pottery itself. Medieval pottery can also demonstrate the extent of trade between regions or countries, as well as patterns of marketing on a local scale. On all of these subjects documentary evidence may be partial or absent.

Fundamental to the analysis of any of these problems is the establishment of datable sequences of types. Excavations of medieval sites provide few coins, and the main evidence for dating different types of pottery is their association with structures such as castles, palaces or defences which can be dated by other means. Other types are themselves dated by their association with these vessels in cesspits, wells or occupation layers. Uncertainties are however introduced by such factors as the unequal lengths of time which different types of vessel may be kept before being broken, and by the differing rates of evolution of styles of pottery-making under the erratic influences of fashion or technological change. There are still few examples of medieval pottery which can be dated more accurately than to within thirty or forty years. The discussion of the development of pottery styles would, however, not be possible without at least an outline framework of reasonably close dating. Such dates as are given in this book should therefore be treated as a guide or as a hypothesis rather than as a statement of established fact: many of them will probably need revision as a result of further research.

2
Saxo-Norman pottery
(AD 850 to 1150)

In the ninth century the growth of several towns such as York, Ipswich, London, Canterbury and *Hamwic* (Southampton) reflected the trade already developing between England and northern Europe. The conquest of part of England by Viking armies, and the subsequent influx of Scandinavian settlers, also stimulated both inland and overseas trade. It is, at least in part, a consequence of these developments that during this period several new types of pottery were introduced into England, whose manufacture used techniques which had been lost with the collapse of industrialised pottery-making at the end of the Roman period.

East Anglia

The hand-made vessels in use in England up to 850 (of which the most 'industrialised' was *Ipswich ware* (**1,** 1-3) made in or near Ipswich) were replaced in eastern England by three main types. These were made on a fast wheel (see Glossary) and usually fired in technically developed kilns. Their introduction marks the beginning of a new stage in English ceramic history. These types are together termed *Saxo-Norman,* since they lasted without a break in production until marked changes took place in the industry in the twelfth century, and they dominated the markets of eastern England and the Midlands for the next three centuries, though showing throughout this period a marked conservatism of both form and decoration. Each was first named after its type-site, but all were made in more than one centre.

St Neots-type ware is a soft ware with black or red-brown surfaces, tempered with crushed shell probably in the form of fossils from the Oxford clay. All these features suggest that it was probably fired in simple clamp kilns at a temperature below 850C. It had a wide distribution in the Midlands west of the Wash.

The main vessel types are tall cooking pots or jars (**4,** 8-10); bowls, mostly with inturned or flanged rims (**4,** 11-24) and some with hollow 'spouts' for the insertion of wooden handles (**4,** 14); dishes or plates (**5,** 1-9); and lamps. All of these are found in a wide range of sizes. The absence of the spouted pitcher, common to the Thetford- and Stamford-type wares, is due to the fact that this ware was probably too soft to make carriers for liquid. It was not until about 1100, when an increasing amount of sand tempering was used in the fabric, that the handled jugs (**5,** 10-17) began to be made.

These shelly fabrics were common to other hand-made wares made from the middle Saxon period. The true St Neots-type ware represents a refinement of existing pottery-making traditions, superimposing on them for a time distinctive shapes thrown on a fast wheel. From the twelfth century some areas produced debased versions of cooking pots and jugs (**5,** 18), termed *developed St Neots-type wares.*

Thetford-type ware is a hard reduced grey ware tempered with sand, fired to comparatively high temperatures in fully developed kilns, and is widely distributed over Norfolk and Suffolk. Several kiln sites have been found in towns — three in Thetford and others in Ipswich and Norwich — as well as two of a later period in rural areas (Langhale and Grimston).

The characteristic forms of this ware are tall cooking pots or jars (**2,** 3-10; **3,** 1-8), some of them with rouletted decoration (**2,** 4; **3,** 1 and 4); bowls (**3,** 17-20 and 23-4); spouted pitchers with both tubular and U-shaped spouts (**1,** 4-9); storage jars (**2,** 1-2); dishes (**3,** 25-7); costrels (**1,** 10-11); crucibles and lamps. The storage jars are massive vessels with multiple handles, invariably hand-built and decorated with applied bands and stamped motifs — all features copying the relief-band amphorae imported from Badorf in the Rhineland from the ninth century. The spouted pitcher form was also derived from a standard type current over much of northern Europe in this period and had an ancestry in England in the middle Saxon spouted pitchers of Ipswich ware (**1,** 1-3).

Stamford-type ware has a distinctive white or buff fabric, fired in oxidising conditions in contrast to the reduced Thetford-type ware. The finer vessels such as the spouted pitchers and some bowls were covered with a thin yellow or pale green lead glaze, though most of the output was unglazed. This is one of the earliest types of glazed pottery in northern Europe; the technique of glazing was probably reintroduced from the Byzantine countries through France. Kiln sites have been excavated at Stamford, but the several variants found over a wide area in the Midlands and the north-east, commonly for instance in York, can best be explained by the existence of a number of production centres. A recently discovered kiln site at Stamford itself, operating in the later ninth century, was producing a range of forms which included bowls, spouted pitchers, cooking pots and large storage vessels. The last two forms were glazed and decorated with red paint, showing continental influences at this time.

A high level of industrialisation is indicated by the large number of standard forms of this ware, produced in a range of sizes. These include the glazed spouted pitcher with one or three handles (**6**, 1-7), a type widely traded over the whole of England; jars (**6**, 8-9); cooking pots (**6**, 12-14); bowls (**6**, 10-11; **7**, 1-11) with the rim either rouletted (**7**, 3, 7 and 10) or with applied thumbed strips (**7**, 1); lamps, crucibles and lids. Some of these types possibly date from the late ninth century, though they are more commonly found in eleventh- and twelfth-century contexts.

Towards the end of the eleventh century the jug form (**7**, 12-13) was introduced for the first time in England. In the early twelfth century a new version was produced (*developed Stamford ware*), with jugs, bottles and cooking pots covered with a bright mottled green glaze, and the jugs further decorated with applied strips and multiple combed lines (**7**, 14-17). Two kilns producing these wares have been excavated in Stamford itself.

The Midlands and the north

Kilns or distinctive types of wheel-thrown pottery have now been found in or near the five Scandinavian *burhs:* Stamford, Lincoln, Leicester, Nottingham and Derby. Other kilns have also recently been found at Stafford, Northampton and Torksey.

At *Leicester* a kiln of the tenth or eleventh century made unglazed cooking pots (**3**, 12) and pitchers or storage vessels. A pottery industry at *Lincoln* was well established by the tenth century with at least one kiln making high-quality wheel-thrown, shell-gritted pottery in standardised forms (mainly bowls and cooking pots) in the early eleventh century (**27**, 1-2). At *Nottingham* tall cooking pots with splashes of glaze caused by the use of powdered galena (*splashed-glaze ware*) were made in at least three kilns, in or just outside the city, in the tenth and eleventh centuries. This type is also found in Lincoln, York and elsewhere, suggesting either a wide trade in these wares or else the existence of more than one production centre. Another type of wheel-thrown sandy ware, similar to unglazed Stamford-type ware, was also made in *Northampton* from the mid tenth to eleventh centuries. The forms included cooking pots with flat bases (**3**, 9-10), bowls (**3**, 21-2), but no spouted pitchers. *Torksey ware,* a type similar to Thetford-type ware and dating to the tenth and eleventh centuries, was also made at Torksey, Lincolnshire, where several kilns have been excavated. This is found over much of north-east England, including York. The forms included bowls (**4**, 3-5) and cooking pots (**4**, 1-2) of standard shape.

At Whitby, North Yorkshire, and the monasteries of Monkwearmouth and Jarrow wheel-thrown pottery in fine micaceous fabric (*Whitby-type ware:* **4,** 6) was in use before the Danish raids of 875. Another industry at York produced wheel-thrown pottery in the tenth and eleventh centuries in a hard gritted fabric (*York ware*) in forms which include mainly tall cooking pots with some spouted pitchers and bowls. At Chester a distinctive type of pottery was being made in or near the town by the tenth century (*Chester-type ware*), the forms including tall cooking pots with convex bases and rouletted decoration (**4,** 7), bowls, and possibly storage jars and spouted pitchers, all in a hard oxidised brown sandy fabric. This type was widely traded through much of the Midlands in the tenth century and was probably made at a number of different centres.

The south of England

There is little evidence that the Saxo-Norman pottery industry in the areas already described had any influence on the pottery-making in the south of England. Wheel-thrown wares were made on an industrial scale at several centres from the tenth century, most of them again in important towns.

Winchester ware is a type of high-quality decorated pottery with a yellow lead glaze, produced from 950 to 1100 probably in Winchester itself. It represents a different though parallel tradition to the contemporary Stamford-type wares. Few complete profiles of any of the vessel types have been found, but they include spouted pitchers (eighty per cent of the finds) with opposed handles and convex bases (**8,** 3-4); pitchers without spouts (**8,** 1 and 5); jars with handles but no spout (**8,** 2); bottles or flasks, of which a complete vessel (**8,** 9) is a remarkably close skeuomorph of a leather prototype — even to the extent of showing stitch-holes and carrying straps; and cups (**8,** 8), bowls (**8,** 6-7), lids (probably for jars) and sprinklers. Other forms, introduced probably towards the end of the series, included jugs and tripod pitchers.

Many of these vessels were highly decorated with incised, stamped or rouletted motifs, or applied strips. In the early twelfth century a new type appeared (*developed Winchester ware*) which is represented by jugs and larger pitchers with green glazes and sometimes with applied criss-cross strips of red-firing clay (cf. the similar development at both Stamford and Oxford).

Parallel with the production of wheel-thrown Winchester ware were the glazed tripod pitchers (**8,** 10), large globular vessels, built by hand, which were in use from the late tenth century. Variants on this shape were to become common over much of the south of England in the eleventh, twelfth and early thirteenth centuries. The three-handled spouted pitcher from Winchester illustrated, of *c.* 1100, is glazed yellow and decorated with roller-stamped lines and horizontal and vertical applied thumbed strips. These vessels must have functioned not as tableware (for which purpose the Winchester ware may have been used by the well-to-do) but as containers or carriers for either water or wine.

Recent work has now identified an earlier type of wheel-thrown pottery from Winchester, comprising cooking pots made in a sandy fabric and dating from the ninth and early tenth centuries.

Exeter ware. A kiln in Exeter making buff oxidised pottery, previously dated to the thirteenth or fourteenth century, has only recently been recognised as being broadly of late tenth or eleventh-century date. It produced only a limited range of forms: mainly small and medium-sized cooking pots with convex bases (**8,** 19-21) and decorated handled jars (**8,** 18) — but no spouted pitchers. The vessels are competently thrown on a fast wheel, and several are partially covered with a green or yellow glaze.

Portchester-type ware is a hard sandy wheel-thrown pottery of the tenth and eleventh centuries from Portchester and nearby. The forms included cooking pots with convex bases and horizontal rilling or rouletted decoration on the shoulders or rim (**8,** 11-12); bowls; and flat dishes (**8,** 14). A single small spouted pitcher with orange glaze and with decoration of rouletted applied strips from Portchester (**8,** 13) may be a product of this industry (showing distinct affinities with Michelmersh ware), though it may well be an import from northern France.

Michelmersh ware is an unglazed type in a smooth brown sandy fabric, dating to the tenth or eleventh century. Forms include globular spouted pitchers (**8,** 15) with single handles, applied cordons at the shoulders and stamped and rouletted decoration; cooking pots (**8,** 16); and dishes (**8,** 17).

Other types of cooking pot of the Saxo-Norman period made on a fast wheel are known from *Winchester* (**22,** 7) from the eleventh century and have also for instance been identified at *Cheddar.*

Conclusion

The overall picture in the north-east, Midlands and eastern England in the late Saxon period is therefore one of the widespread use of high-quality wheel-thrown pottery, of which the Stamford and Thetford varieties were the most common and showed the greatest degree of industrialisation. At lease some of these centres were producing pottery in England before the Danish raids from *c.* 875, though most were encouraged as a result of the trading activities of the Scandinavian settlers.

Similar pottery came somewhat later in the south of England, but its manufacture was well established in a number of centres by the eleventh century.

The fact that most of these industries were located in towns probably reflects the expansion of urban markets over much of England from the late ninth century, as well as the attempts by the later Saxon kings to limit trading to towns by legislation.

The emergence of these new industries is significant. All employed techniques of a higher degree of sophistication than had hitherto been used in these regions, and all produced a range of vessel forms already widely made in northern Europe. It seems likely that both the forms and the manufacturing techniques were introduced by immigrant potters attracted both by the large populations in the east and north-east and by the growth of towns over all of England in the tenth century.

The general differences in form between the rounded or baggy types in the south and the taller shapes made in the east and north-east also suggest that these potters came from two different areas — from the Rhineland to East Anglia, Lincolnshire and Yorkshire in the ninth and early tenth centuries, and probably from northern France to the south of England in the later tenth and eleventh centuries.

3
Medieval pottery
(1100 to 1500)

Twelfth century

Over much of eastern and north-eastern England the long-standing urban-based pottery industry of the later Saxon period declined, giving way in the twelfth century to smaller-scale pottery-making centres outside the towns. In many areas the developed techniques of throwing and kiln construction introduced in the ninth century were lost and the earlier standardised pottery types were replaced by hand-made cooking pots of generally broader and squatter form, as well as by debased forms of jugs. Shell-tempered clays were widely used to make pottery fired to low temperatures in unstructured clamp kilns — a tradition which was to continue in many areas until the thirteenth or even the fourteenth century. These local centres generally depended on the nearest urban or village market for the distribution of their products, and their natural development gave rise to the regional diversification of types which is so marked a feature of the medieval pottery industry until well into the sixteenth century.

In only a few centres was there any continuity of production on an industrial scale. One of these was at Stamford, where the high-quality developed Stamford ware continued to be manufactured throughout the twelfth and thirteenth centuries, when the potters are thought to have moved to Nottingham.

A similar breakdown of traditions of wheel-thrown pottery, with a consequent development of regional types, can also be seen in the south. Both the glazed and unglazed types already mentioned, with the exception of the tripod pitchers, ceased production around 1100, though semi-industrialised pottery-making may have continued in or near Winchester throughout the twelfth century. Over most of England the staple product of the early medieval potters was the cooking pot, together with the tripod and spouted pitchers in southern England, and different forms of jugs in all areas from the twelfth century onwards. In many areas simple lead glazes began to be used on the jugs, and in the Midlands on cooking pots also (e.g. the splashed-glaze ware of Nottingham).

Thirteenth and fourteenth centuries

The proliferation of regional styles gave rise to a wide range of vessel types. By the fourteenth century there can have been few areas in the British Isles without their local pottery industry. At the same time techniques of potting improved rapidly: the increasingly common use of sand rather than shell or limestone as a tempering agent made possible the use of a faster wheel, improved throwing techniques and the natural development of taller and narrower shapes. These developments were accompanied by the use of more advanced kilns firing to higher temperatures. Cooking pots, some of them very large, continued to be made throughout this period, though in decreasing quantities in many areas owing to the wider use of bronze or iron cooking vessels. Jugs or pitchers formed a larger proportion of the output of the industry, and it is these which best show the distinct regional variations. Throughout the thirteenth century, and into the fourteenth, these vessels became increasingly lavishly decorated with designs in painted and trailed slips of different colours, with applied ornamentation of human figures, animals, faces and abstract designs, and sometimes with combinations of different types of glazes — a trend which paralleled and was in many cases influenced by similar developments in western Europe and Scandinavia.

During the fourteenth century the pottery industry in most of England seems to have suffered an almost complete collapse. This must, at least in part, have been due to the series of plagues in the early fourteenth century (of which the Black Death in 1348 was the most virulent) and the social and economic changes which these brought about. Pottery in this period is difficult to date, but its general rarity may well mean that by the end of the century the decorated and other good-quality pottery had in many areas ceased being produced.

Fifteenth century

Much pottery of this period is plainly utilitarian and of low quality. By the middle of the century, however, several areas, particularly in the Midlands and around London, had begun producing basic household wares on an industrial scale and in shapes common to wide areas of the country. New and distinctive types of vessels such as large 'bung-hole' pitchers, skillets, bowls, plates and cups, as well as the more usual small jugs, many of these in graded sizes, began to be made by the industry. The development of some types (such as the Tudor green wares in Surrey) could possibly even be attributed to an influx of potters from the Continent.

4
Some regional types: Oxford and London

The general trends outlined in the last chapter can be illustrated only by considering some regional styles in each period. The development of pottery types from two areas — Oxford, ninth to fourteenth centuries, and London, ninth to fifteenth centuries — are illustrated in detail, since their evolution reflects similar developments in other regions.

Oxford region

Saxo-Norman period. A number of excavations in Oxford over the last few years have considerably clarified the ceramic sequence. The local pottery tradition begins with a series of handmade cooking pots, shallow dishes and bowls made with clay tempered with much shell and limestone. These are first made in the late eighth or early ninth century, though they continue in use into the eleventh century. Although widely distributed in the region they were probably made in or near Oxford. Pottery of this type is also found in early levels at Staines and London, indicating the use of the Thames as a trade route in the ninth century. Another type of pottery from Northampton is also found at this early period.

This type was replaced during the tenth and early eleventh century by wheel-thrown St Neots-type ware which was probably introduced from the east Midlands by Danish settlers and subsequently made locally. These included bowls (**9**, 3), platters and cooking pots (**9**, 1-2, 4 and 7), as well as jugs (**5**, 12) from about 1100. Throughout the Saxon period a number of English and continental pottery types were clearly brought from further afield, such as from Northampton, Stamford, Southampton and other parts of Wessex. Although the eleventh century was one of economic recession, a flourishing local industry (mentioned in Domesday Book) was centred at *Bladon,* and a village industry of the twelfth century at *Ascot Doilly* was making shelly pottery from local clays, including jugs (**11**, 6), bowls (**11**, 5) and pipkins (**11**, 7).

Other forms included the distinctive straight-sided cooking pots (**9**, 11-12) in use from the mid eleventh century to *c.* 1200, and baggy spouted pitchers with simple stamped or combed decoration (**9**, 5-6). Both these were made on a slow wheel or turntable.

Early medieval period. Throughout the eleventh, twelfth and thirteenth centuries the cooking pots developed squatter and broader forms (**9,** 8-10, 16-20), making increasing use of sand as a tempering agent, and becoming thinner and harder as throwing and firing techniques improved. The twelfth century also saw the introduction of large pans (**9,** 14), as well as large storage jars, of which **11,** 1 is an example of the thirteenth century. Both are local developments of types which have an ancestry in the Saxon period.

Large jugs in a shelly fabric (**10,** 11) were made in the late eleventh and twelfth centuries, when the first local glazed types appeared. These were tripod pitchers (**10,** 1-4 and 6), jugs without spouts (**10,** 7-8) and small spouted bottles (**10,** 5), all made in a white- or buff-firing clay tempered with sand, and having a thin yellow glaze. The tripod pitchers were clearly introduced into Oxford from the Winchester area, where they are known from a century earlier. The Oxford examples have knife-trimmed convex bases and, unlike the Winchester examples, were probably thrown on a fast wheel, the outflaring neck of each vessel subsequently built up by hand from slabs or coils. A series of vessels ranging in size between the large spouted pitchers with feet and the smaller jugs without these features was probably made at the same (unknown) centre.

By the late twelfth century contemporary developments elsewhere (e.g. at Stamford, Winchester and London) are mirrored in the use of strips of red-firing clay on the body of the pots (**10,** 9) and the addition of green colouring to the earlier yellow glazes (**10,** 3).

Thirteenth and fourteenth centuries. The baggy tripod pitchers of the twelfth century lasted into the early thirteenth and were the forerunners of wide-bodied jugs made in a harder fired sandy fabric (**10,** 10 and 12; **12,** 1-2 and 4-8), often decorated with lines and dots of white slip (**12,** 4) or with painted stripes of red-brown slip (**12,** 2 and 5-7). These and similar large jugs from London (**14,** 8-10) and elsewhere seem to reflect contemporary fashion in the south. Another Oxford type of the early or mid thirteenth century is a large jug with convex base, decorated with swirling lines of white slip, glazed either yellow (**12,** 3) or green.

In the later thirteenth century these gave way to taller jugs decorated with complex motifs of applied scales and strips of brown or buff clay, small face masks and other designs. Characteristic of Oxford are the sharply carinated jugs decorated either with strips of red-firing clay and with a thin yellow lead glaze (**13,** 1-4) or with more complex motifs of lines, scales and petals in white and red slip, and with green glazes (**13,** 9); jugs, imitating French forms and decoration (**13,** 5); 'puzzle-jugs' decorated with applied scales, strips of red-firing clay and stags' heads (**13,** 10); and corrugated beakers with face masks (**13,** 11). Many of these types were made at *Brill,* 16 kilometres (10 miles) north-east of Oxford, from the mid thirteenth century.

In the fourteenth century the highly decorated jugs were probably supplanted by the simple but elegant baluster jugs (**13,** 6-8). They are highly fired and thinly glazed vessels with simple painted stripes of white- or red-firing slip. Some of the cooking pots and storage jars in the thirteenth and early fourteenth centuries became quite large (**11,** 1-3, 8-10) but in the later period were largely replaced by metal cauldrons.

Later medieval period. The general lack of finds of the later fourteenth and fifteenth centuries — a time when the town was in decline — makes it difficult to define the ceramic types of this period. However, some jugs with much mottled green glaze were in use in this period, and the kilns at Brill produced a range of smaller jugs with carinated profiles (**13,** 15-18). Other types of vessels included small bottles or cruets (**13,** 13-14 and 19-22), and mugs or cups of various forms, some of them glazed green (**13,** 12 and 23-4), others in the later part of the fifteenth century imitating the Cistercian-type wares of the north Midlands and Yorkshire (**13,** 25-8).

London region

The primacy of London amongst the towns of medieval England, with the consequent high demand by its citizens for basic household goods, must have encouraged around its periphery many pottery production centres. The recent progress made in the study of pottery in London has led to the identification both of new types and, more importantly, the place of manufacture of these and of types already known.

Saxon and early medieval periods. The earliest pottery type identified from London is chaff-tempered ware, which ranges in date probably from the seventh century or earlier to the ninth century. This is succeeded, possibly as early as the late eighth century, by the ubiquitous 'late Saxon shelly ware', which analysis has determined was made near Oxford and shipped down-river to London, probably as an item in a two-way trade. The range of forms includes cooking pots, spouted pitchers (**14,** 1), lamps and hollow handled bowls which are similar in shape to those of Thetford-type ware (**1** and **2**). In the late tenth century these types were joined by similar vessels using the same range of forms but made in a sandy fabric ('Early Medieval sandy ware') which was common over much of southern England. Both types lasted well into the eleventh century.

In the eleventh century, however, a greater variety of types is found in London, including a range of imports, Thetford-type ware and others from Surrey and the East Midlands.

Twelfth to fourteenth centuries. In the twelfth and thirteenth centuries large numbers of jugs and cooking pots from London in an unglazed hard grey sandy fabric (**14,** 3-4) were being made at *Elstree,* Hertfordshire. Another unknown centre of this period (probably in Essex) was producing a range of bulbous jugs with yellow glaze, many of them with painted diagonal, horizontal or criss-cross stripes of different coloured slips (**14,** 8-10). These were made in a large range of sizes, indicating a level of industrialisation unusual for the period. Tripod pitchers (**14,** 5-7) are not uncommon and appear in the mid twelfth century; the type represented by **14,** 6 must have lasted well into the thirteenth century.

In probably the early thirteenth century the arrival in England of fine decorated jugs in a white fabric from Rouen in France gave rise to a flourishing industry near London producing copies, possibly made by Frenchmen, in red-firing clay (**15,** 1-6). An interesting jug (**15,** 7) with several of these features shows a hunting scene, with men on horseback, hounds and stags, applied in a thick white slip. In the later fourteenth century various other types of jug in a red fabric, decorated with white slip lines (**15,** 11-14) and with a clear lead glaze, were also being produced.

Late thirteenth and fourteenth centuries. The source of supply for pottery in the twelfth and early thirteenth centuries was from in or near London itself, from Hertfordshire and Essex, with a small proportion from Kent (primarily *Limpsfield*). It seems likely that a source of supply in southern Hertfordshire or Essex will be found for the London-type jugs in particular. In the mid and later thirteenth century, however, a new source of supply was found in Surrey, particularly *Kingston-upon-Thames*. Kilns here produced high quality pottery, known generally as *Surrey white wares,* using the white-firing clay of the Reading Beds. These soon dominated the London market. The jugs assumed a variety of shapes and sometimes quite enormous sizes (**16,** 3-4), and some of them were decorated with intricate patterns of trailed white, red and green slip (**16,** 1-8), applied scales and stamped pellets (**16,** 4-5 and 8).

Many of these showed stylistic features such as the rod handles with spurs (**16**, 2-4 and 7-8) and the angular shapes (**16**, 8), which were derived from northern French prototypes. A jug of this type (**16**, 7), with an added decoration of a heraldic beast in white slip on a red-painted background, has a clear ancestry in two imported northern French vessels recently found in Southampton and in Surrey. Another characteristic type is the 'face-on-front' jug (**17**, 1-4) with arms clutching either the chin or a buckle on the front of the 'belly'. Kingston was also the main source of jugs of various shapes with decorations of impressed motifs of wheatsheaves, wheat-ears, fleur-de-lys, horseshoes and coats of arms (**17**, 5-7), with undecorated jugs of the same shape (**17**, 8 and 20-1). Cooking pots and bowls in standard shapes (**18**, 1-6), some with green glaze on the inside, were also produced in this white ware.

At the same time, from the late thirteenth century, other jugs in a red-firing sandy ware were made in large numbers at an unknown centre. Some were covered with a white slip in imitation of the apparently more pleasing Surrey white wares. One common type made at *Mill Green* in Essex is represented by jugs of three different shapes (**15**, 8-10) in a hard red fabric, with an overall white slip and green glaze. Another class of undecorated jugs used for drinking was produced in several graded sizes (**16**, 9-14). The largest of these, including the 'tulip-necked baluster' pitcher (**16**, 9), have an overall white slip and small bib of clear glaze (**16**, 9-10); the middle sizes (**16**, 11-12) have glaze but no slip; and the smallest two (**16**, 13-14) have neither glaze nor slip. Two straight-sided unglazed jugs (**16**, 15-16) in the same ware show the same characteristics: the larger one has an overall white slip, the smaller one is without it.

Late medieval period. There is much evidence to suggest that the types of decorated jugs of the thirteenth to the early fourteenth centuries ceased to be made over much of England after the middle of the century. In contrast, however, the jugs from London show a more or less continuous development until the sixteenth century. The Surrey white ware industry supplied most of the London market from a number of kiln sites during the later fourteenth and fifteenth centuries. In the mid fourteenth century the industry at Kingston seems to have given way to one, located near the Surrey/Hampshire border, which supplied more than half of London's pottery, though other industries supplied smaller amounts. All of these produced jugs of various sizes, invariably (except for the products from Cheam) with a thick green glaze. Cooking pots were produced throughout the period but in increasingly small quantities. The widespread adoption of bronze cooking vessels which led to this trend also gave rise to a number of pottery skeuomorphs, with angular handles (**18**, 7), long tripod feet, or both features (**18**, 7-8).

From the later fourteenth century the shape of bronze jugs (**17**, 19) also had a strong influence on their ceramic equivalents (**17**, 12-18). Some of these were made at Kingston-upon-Thames in the late fourteenth century and most types were produced in graded sizes. Other jugs of this period were covered with rows of applied scales (**17**, 9-10). Large bung-hole pitchers with red-painted decoration (**19**,1) also became common, and face-on-front jugs (**19**, 2) continued in production. Another source which supplied London with pottery in the late fourteenth and fifteenth centuries was St Albans, where small jugs with a thin green glaze (**17**, 10) were made.

Other forms made at this period include unglazed retorts (**18**, 19-20) and crucibles (**18**, 21-2), and green-glazed mugs (**18**, 15), urinals (**18**, 16), costrels (**18**,17), a torch (**18**, 18), and large platters (**18**, 9).

In the fifteenth century a large-scale pottery industry flourished at *Cheam,* where a kiln of the mid fifteenth century produced jugs in graded sizes with carinated (**19**, 9-13) or barrel-shaped (**19**, 3-8) profiles. These had a hard off-white fabric and were only thinly glazed, and some were decorated with broad swirling lines of painted red slip (**19**, 7-9). Other forms include bowls (**19**, 15-17), plates (**15**, 18) and cooking pots (**15**, 14). Later in the century at least one other kiln site at Cheam was producing small jugs and bung-hole pitchers (**19**, 22-4) in a highly fired red fabric, many with painted decoration of abstract floral motifs in white slip.

With the production of these wares this branch of the white-ware industry in Surrey virtually disappeared. Another branch, at Farnborough Hill, however, began to make a range of thin-walled vessels with thick green glazes from the late fifteenth century. These are known as *Tudor green ware,* the most distinctive examples of which are a series of lobed and corrugated mugs and cups (**19**, 25-7). It is possible that the superior techniques required for their manufacture (which included, for the first time in English medieval pottery, a biscuit firing stage) were introduced directly from France at this time. Examples of this ware were widely distributed over England and supplied a demand for new types of ceramic products in the later fifteenth century, to which the manufacture of the Cistercian-type wares in the north Midlands and Yorkshire was a similar response.

5
Some regional types: other areas

Winchester and Southampton

Large-scale excavations in both these towns have produced much medieval pottery; good sequences of types are therefore available, especially for the period up to the end of the thirteenth century.

In the *Southampton* region, at middle Saxon *Hamwic* and in the medieval town, continental influences have always predominated. In the late Saxon period local types include small hand-built cooking pots with rounded bases (**20**, 1-6) made in a flint and limestone gritted fabric in the tenth century. By the late tenth century these developed into the distinctive hand-made *scratch-marked wares* (**20**, 11-14) fired in clamp kilns. These were made in many sizes and lasted well into the thirteenth century with little change in shape. Shelly wares and flint-gritted (**20**, 7-10) sandy wares were made in flatter forms from at least the twelfth century. All these types are the products of distinct but overlapping traditions, each with a long life, and each showing little tendency to change once it had started.

At *Winchester,* however, wheel-thrown cooking pots with angular convex bases (**22**, 1 and 7) were made concurrently with hand-made types with rounded bases (**22**, 6) from the eleventh century. These more advanced types are a further example of the intrusive ceramic influences which produced Winchester ware and the Winchester tripod pitchers and which reflect the dominance of Winchester as a regional centre.

In both places spouted (**22**, 3-4; **20**, 18) and tripod pitchers were in use at an early period. At Southampton the unusual green-glazed vessel (**20**, 18) of the eleventh century, with rouletted decoration and applied thumbed strips, shows French influences but is also similar to the Winchester tripod pitchers (**8**, 10). In the thirteenth and fourteenth centuries the local pottery industry, which produced jugs with green glazes (**21**, 14-16), was very much eclipsed by the imported fine wares coming from both the north and south-west of France as a by-product of the wine trade. Jugs from other regions found in Southampton included examples of *West Sussex ware* (**21**, 12-13), bulbous vessels with yellow and green glazes and applied decoration, possibly made at *Binstead;* and *Laverstock ware*. Decorated jugs found in Winchester of this period include an example with moulded faces and stamped red-painted oval areas (**22,** 11), possibly made at Laverstock, and another showing a figure with arms holding a large sword moulded in high relief and with contrasting red- and buff-firing clays (**22,** 12).

The south-west

Over much of this area, including Wales, little or no pottery seems to have been used in the Saxon period. The west of Cornwall, however, with its contacts with Ireland, developed a distinctive type — the *bar-lug* cooking pot, in use from the ninth to the eleventh centuries (**23,** 7). Vessels of this type were hand-built in slabs, with the addition of two protective lugs covering horizontal handles at the rim to enable the pot to be hung over a fire.

At *Castle Neroche,* Somerset, the absence of local pottery caused the Norman lord to import a French potter who made cooking pots, spouted pitchers and storage jars in shapes common to Normandy (**23,** 8-9), but made from local clays. From the eleventh into the thirteenth century cooking pots with convex bases, as well as wide-mouthed round-bellied jugs (**23,** 10-11) in the same fabrics and sometimes with a thin wash of glaze, were made over a wide area. The former are of a distinctive type with a dished rim (**23,** 4-6). Tripod pitchers, derived from the Winchester and Oxford types, are common in a belt from Dorset to Gloucester (**23,** 1-3) and persisted into the thirteenth or early fourteenth century.

French influences are apparent on many of the jugs of the thirteenth and fourteenth centuries, for instance those of the thirteenth century from *Exeter* (**23,** 12-13), and in others made at *Ham Green* near Bristol (**23,** 14-16), whose products had a wide distribution over the west of England and south Wales. Some of these jugs, decorated with trailed slip figures, and in one case with a free-standing figure of a knight with a shield, also show strong influences from the Midlands.

French influence is also seen in the products of two kiln sites of this period: at Rye, East Sussex, and Laverstock, near Salisbury. At *Rye* the jug types included broad forms with impressed and stamped designs (**24,** 1), bulbous forms with marked parrot-beak spouts (**24,** 6-7) of south-western French type, and others with red-painted decoration (**24,** 2-5). Some jugs have scratched designs of figures, boats, animals and a scene from a tournament (**24,** 12-15), a type of ornamentation rare on English medieval pottery. Other products included skillets (**24,** 8), bowls with handles (**24,** 9-10), shallow handled cups (**24,** 11) and cooking pots.

At *Laverstock* jugs were the main product and evolved in style through the thirteenth century from baggy shapes (**24,** 16-18) with curvilinear or foliage designs to taller forms, either with or without parrot-beak spouts· (**24,** 19-20), and with applied and stamped stripes, pellets and red-painted lines. Anthropomorphic jugs of the 'face-on-front' type or with impressed face-mask medallions on the side were also produced. Other products of the kilns included costrels, aquamaniles, small jugs (**24,** 21), bottles, mortars, curfews, lamps, lids and money boxes, as well as ridge tiles, chimneypots, louvres and water pipes. The range of products and their high quality must reflect the proximity of the large urban markets of Salisbury and Winchester.

The Midlands and Yorkshire
Early medieval period. The pottery which supplanted the Saxo-Norman types developed markedly regional styles, yet there is in some places evidence of continuity of both styles and techniques into later periods. In *Lincoln* the industrial production of standardised shelly pottery (**27,** 1-2) in the tenth and eleventh centuries gave way after *c.* 1100 to less standardised forms which developed until the fourteenth century (**27,** 3-4). There was some continuity in the traditions of glazing pottery, however, at both Lincoln and *Nottingham,* where the splashed-glaze ware of the tenth and eleventh centuries was succeeded in the twelfth century by *developed splashed-glaze ware,* with cooking pots, bowls and now jugs with a speckled green instead of a yellow glaze. This ware is found over much of Lincolnshire and south Yorkshire.

In *York* flatter shapes of cooking pot had developed by the twelfth century, though elsewhere in Yorkshire, such as at the kilns at *Upper Heaton* (**29,** 1-9), the earlier shapes were still being made in the thirteenth century. As elsewhere, these examples point to the simultaneous development of different industrial traditions.

Thirteenth and fourteenth centuries. The jugs of the north of England from the thirteenth century show characteristics which are not shared by those in the south. In the twelfth and thirteenth centuries the north-east was ceramically more advanced than the rest of the country, except perhaps for the London area, and the developments here were probably due to the continuation and spread of the forms first developed with Stamford-type ware. At Lincoln the developed splashed-glaze ware of Nottingham, probably also made at Lincoln (**27,** 5-6), was succeeded in the late thirteenth and fourteenth centuries by a range of green-glazed jugs (*Lincoln ware*) with tall waisted necks and sometimes twisted handles (**27,** 7-11) and by flat-based cooking pots (**27,** 12-13). Similar green-glazed jugs

(**26,** 1 and 6-7), as well as cooking pots (**26,** 2-4), also developed at Nottingham, where several kiln sites of this period, situated both inside and just outside the medieval city wall, have been excavated.

A distinct regional type of decorated jug is found in *Leicester* and *Coventry* (**25,** 1-3 and 8-9). The surfaces of these vessels were often covered with abstract or floral motifs in applied or trailed slip, or with figures with brooches (**25,** 8) in trailed slip and incised lines. This latter motif was copied widely, similar types occurring in Cheshire, London and Bristol (at the Ham Green kilns: **23,** 14-16). The tripod cauldron from Leicester of the thirteenth century (**25,** 7), copying metal prototypes, is unusual, though similar to finds from London (**18,** 7-8) and other places.

Several pottery industries developed in the south Midlands, the largest of which was at *Nuneaton,* where over fifty kilns, many of them coal-fired, have been excavated, and which produced a wide range of forms into the late medieval period. A village industry at *Lyveden,* Northamptonshire, is important because not only kilns but complete workshops have been excavated. Jug types from East Anglia are represented by the large vessel from Cambridge with white slip painted on to a brick-red body (**25,** 10), and by several vessels with an overall white slip, through which designs have been scratched, with a yellow glaze (**25,** 11-12).

Another distinctive northern type was the jug with a long tubular spout attached to the shoulder of the vessel, with a plain or decorated strut between spout and neck (**26,** 8; **28,** 8 and 10-12). It is this type which shows the greatest similarity to the jugs of developed Stamford ware (**7,** 16). Undecorated spouted jugs are for example common in York and were made in kilns at *Doncaster, Winksley* (**28,** 8) and *Scarborough* (**28,** 10-12), amongst others. The type was also sometimes combined with faces and beards, the latter often joined to the shoulder of the vessel forming subsidiary handles at the sides. Kilns making these types include one near York and others at Scarborough, Doncaster, *Nottingham* (**26,** 8) and *Grimston,* Norfolk (**26,** 10-11). Free-standing figures of knights on horseback or other figures (**28,** 11; **26,** 8) were also used, a type often called the *Nottingham knight jug.* These were, however, probably made at several places in the north Midlands, including Scarborough and Nottingham, as well as at Ham Green, Bristol.

Pottery vessels from kilns operating at this period near the east coast were traded to many areas in northern Europe and Scandinavia. These included plain or bearded jugs of *Grimston ware,* decorated with arms and painted red lines (**26,** 10-11) in a reduced grey fabric, which were traded from King's Lynn; jugs decorated with trailed slip from *Toynton All Saints,* Lincolnshire (**26,** 12); and decorated jugs of *Scarborough ware* (**28,** 10-12) with an oxidised red sandy fabric. All these are found on many sites both on the east coast and across the North Sea. Potters or pottery from the Scarborough industry also provided the stimulus for the beginnings of pottery-making in Scotland in the thirteenth century. A kiln site of this period near *Colstoun* in south-east Scotland made face jugs similar to those from Scarborough.

The decorated pottery from *York* shows a greater variety than from any other area in the north, reflecting once again the importance of a large urban market in stimulating the production of a variety of high-quality pottery. Vessels with a white fabric were being made at Brandsby, 20 kilometres (12½ miles) to the north, and at a site in or near York itself, and other types include *East Pennine gritty ware* and *Humber ware* from Doncaster. The different use of coloured slips and glazes, slip trailing, and applied pellets, scales and floral motifs on jugs (**28,** 3-4) reflects a similar range of decoration on pottery from centres in the south of England.

Other pottery-making centres in Yorkshire included *West Cowick* (fourteenth and fifteenth centuries) and *Upper Heaton* (thirteenth century). The latter produced mainly round and open cooking pots (**29,** 1-5), with only a few jugs (**29,** 6 and 9), suggesting an industry without large urban markets. An unusual decorated skillet (**29,** 8), copying metal prototypes, was also made here. Vessels in an off-white fabric were made at Winksley (**28,** 7-9), the main interest of which lies in its production of yellow-glazed jugs of squat form, with decoration of complex rouletting (**28,** 7 and 9) thought to derive from similar motifs used in southern Holland.

In the north-west pottery kilns have been found inside the town walls of Rhuddlan (mid thirteenth century) and Chester (fourteenth century), as well as at Audlem (thirteenth century) and at Ashton (fourteenth century), the latter producing mainly decorated jugs.

Fifteenth century. In the late fourteenth and fifteenth centuries jugs became plainer, though still large and with green glazes (**28,** 6). In common with other areas, however, it is difficult to date pottery in this period. A type common to the Midlands, known as *Midland purple ware,* current in the early fifteenth century, includes small jugs (**26,** 13-15), costrels and other vessels, nearly all unglazed. These were fired almost to the point of fusion, giving a purple sheen to the surface of the vessels. This development reflects the concentration on quantity and utility rather than quality, which is also seen for instance at Cheam, London.

Another distinctive type of vessel produced from the mid fifteenth century is *Cistercian-type ware*, so called as a result of its recognition on monastic sites in Yorkshire. This type consists of mainly cups, mugs and beakers (**29,** 13-20) with one or more handles, most examples of which have a highly fired dark brown or purple fabric with a rich brown glaze. Some were also decorated with trailed lines, pads or other motifs such as stags' heads (**29,** 18-20) in white slip. The small proportion of these vessels with white fabric and a decoration of dark slip is known as *reversed Cistercian-type ware*. Many of these were made near Wakefield (at *Silcoates* and *Potovens*), but probably also at other sites in the Midlands and Yorkshire. A similar range of vessels, with red fabric and dark green glaze, was also produced in the Oxford region (**13,** 25-28). The production of all these forms reflects a general trend in the late fifteenth century towards the manufacture of new types of pottery over much of England.

6
Kilns

The structures in which pottery was fired were either temporary or semi-permanent. Temporary kilns (or *clamp kilns*) were formed by covering a stack of pots with peat, turves and wood, which was then left to burn without controls. They were consequently used once only and therefore left no recognisable archaeological trace. Their products were soft and reduced and oxidised in patches (cf. St Neots-type ware).

Semi-permanent kilns can be of a variety of types, but their basic elements consisted of an oval or round structure with clay and sometimes stone walls, usually without a dome, and with one or more stoke pits where the fire was produced. The pottery was stacked in the structure, and a temporary covering of clay or sherds of pottery was made for the open top. The atmosphere inside the kiln (oxidising or reducing) can be controlled by various means. Occasionally a platform was provided within the structure, supported by kiln bars, on which the pottery rested.

The excavation of kiln sites is given greater significance by the excavation of ancillary buildings such as workshops. A complete pottery-making site has been excavated at Lyveden, Northamptonshire.

7
Museums

Most museums have collections of local medieval pottery. The following are some of the better collections. All urban excavation units, in particular, will have large collections; most of this material is still in course of active study, but it should eventually find its way to local museums.

Bristol: Bristol City Museum, Queen's Road.

Cambridge: University Museum of Archaeology and Ethnology, Downing Street.

Canterbury: Royal Museum, High Street.

Cardiff: National Museum of Wales, Cathays Park.

Chester: Grosvenor Museum, Grosvenor Street.

Exeter: Rougemont House Museum, Castle Street.

Gloucester: City Museum and Art Gallery, Brunswick Road.

Guildford: Guildford Museum, Castle Arch.

Leicester: Leicestershire Museum and Art Gallery, New Walk.

Lincoln: Lincoln City and County Museum, Broadgate.

London: Museum of London, London Wall, EC2. (The best collection of medieval pottery in England, if not Europe. Unfortunately only a very small proportion is on display, but the rest may be examined on application to the Director.)

London: British Museum, Great Russell Street, WC1. (Good collection and display, some of the material from outside London; also houses a type-series of sherds from kiln excavations.)

London: Victoria and Albert Museum, Cromwell Road, South Kensington, SW7.

Oxford: Ashmolean Museum of Art and Archaeology, Beaumont Street. (Good collection and the best display of any of the museums mentioned.)

Salisbury: Salisbury and South Wiltshire Museum, The King's House, 65 The Close.

Scarborough: Rotunda Museum, Vernon Road.

Southampton: God's House Tower Museum, Tower House, Town Quay. (Best collection of ceramic material imported from the Continent.)

Winchester: Winchester City Museum, The Square.

York: Yorkshire Museum, Museum Gardens.

8
Further reading

The literature on medieval pottery is enormous but confined almost entirely to county archaeological journals, excavation reports and *Medieval Archaeology*. The Medieval Pottery Research Group (c/o Inspectorate of Ancient Monuments, Department of the Environment, Fortress House, 23 Savile Row, London W1X 2HE), publishes a bulletin for subscribers, *Medieval Ceramics,* with articles of both general and specialist interest.

The following general works contain bibliographies themselves:

Barton, K. J. *Medieval Sussex Pottery.* 1979.

Evison, V. I., Hodges, H., and Hurst, J. G. (eds.). *Medieval Pottery from Excavations: Studies presented to G. C. Dunning.* 1974. Contains full bibliographies of G. C. Dunning and on medieval pottery kilns, amongst other topics.

Holdsworth, J. *Selected Pottery Groups, AD 650-1780* [at York]. 1978 (CBA, for York Archaeological Trust).

Hurst, J. G. 'The Pottery' in *The Archaeology of Anglo-Saxon England* (ed. D. M. Wilson). 1976. The most up-to-date survey, covering the period 350-1150 and containing full references. (There is no adequate general survey for the period 1150-1500.)

Jennings, S. *Eighteen Centuries of Pottery from Norwich.* 1981 (Norwich Survey).

Kilmurray, K. *The Pottery Industry of Stamford, Lincs, 850-1250 AD.* 1980 (British Archaeological Reports, 84).

Macpherson-Grant, N. *Local and Imported Wares at Canterbury — late Saxon, Saxo-Norman and Medieval: a provisional guide.* 1981 (Canterbury Archaeological Trust).

Rackham, B. *Medieval English Pottery.* 1948; 2nd edition, ed. J. G. Hurst, 1972.

Plate 1. Unglazed cooking pot (restored) of Chester ware containing hoard of coins deposited *c.* 970 (fig. **4, 7**). (Photo: T. Ward, Grosvenor Museum, Chester)

Plate 2. Tripod pitcher, twelfth century, from Oxford. Decorated with applied thumbed strips, short spouts and handles, and glazed yellow. (Photo: Ashmolean Museum)

Plate 3. Details of handles of tripod pitchers from Oxford, showing decoration with twisted clay ropes and method of attaching handle to body. (Photo: Ashmolean Museum)

Plate 4. Decorated jugs, late thirteenth to fourteenth centuries, from Oxford. All three with applied decoration of red and white slip, and glazed green except for the centre vessel, which is glazed yellow. The right-hand vessel is a 'puzzle-jug'. Drawn left to right in fig. **13**, 9, 2 and 10. (Photo: Ashmolean Museum)

Plate 5. Aquamanile, fourteenth century from Oxford, modelled in the form of a horse and decorated with applied lines and scales. Used for pouring liquids at table. (Photo: Ashmolean Museum)

Plates 6 and 7. A tripod spouted jug and a tripod cauldron both made of bronze in the fourteenth century, illustrating vessel types commonly copied in pottery in the fourteenth and fifteenth centuries. From Oxford. (Photos: Ashmolean Museum)

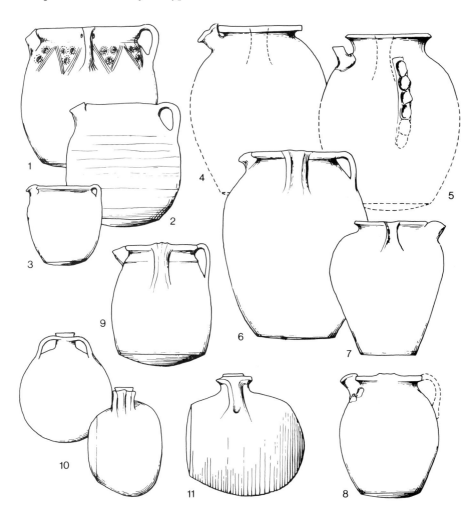

Fig. 1. IPSWICH WARE AND THETFORD-TYPE WARE.
1-3: Ipswich ware spouted pitchers, Ipswich. 1: With incised dec. 4-11: Thetford-type ware. 4-8: Spouted pitchers. 4: Ipswich. 5: With app. dec., Ipswich. 6: Thetford. 7: Colchester. 8: Ely. 9: Spouted pitcher, from Grimston kiln, late 11th to early 12th c. 10-11: Costrels, Thetford. (Drawings: 6, 10: Dunning. 1-5, 7-9, 11: Hurst.)

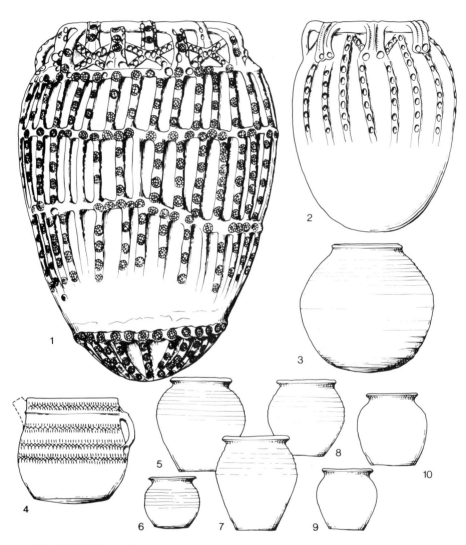

Fig. 2. THETFORD-TYPE WARE.
1-2: Large storage jars (scale 1:10), with multiple handles and dec. with stamped app. strips.
1: Thetford. 2: Norfolk. 3: Cooking pot, Norwich. 4: Handled jar, with rouletted dec.,
Cambs. 5-10: Cooking pots, from Ipswich kiln, all except 6 with flat bases. (Drawings: 1:
Davison. 2: Dunning. 4-10: Hurst. 3: Jope.)

Fig. 3. THETFORD-TYPE WARE.
1-14: Cooking pots. 1-3: From Norwich kiln. 4-5: Thetford. 6: Cambridge. 7-8: Norfolk. 9-10: From Northampton kiln. 11: Suffolk. 12: From Leicester kiln. 13: Rouletted dec., Lincoln. 14: From Langhale kiln. 15-27: Bowls and dishes. 17-19, 22: With hollow handles for insertion of stick. 15-16: From Norwich kiln. 17: From Ipswich kiln. 18: Rouletted dec., Cambridge. 19-20: Thetford. 21-2: From Northampton kiln. 23: Thetford. 24: Cambridge. 25-6: Norfolk. 27: From Grimston kiln. (Drawings: 13: Coppack. 4-5, 8, 19-20, 23: Dunning. 12: Hebditch. 6-7, 11, 14, 17-18, 24-7: Hurst. 1-3, 15-16: Jope. 9-10, 21-2: Williams.)

Fig. 4. TORKSEY WARE, WHITBY-TYPE AND CHESTER-TYPE WARE AND ST
NEOTS-TYPE WARES.
1-5: Cooking pots and bowls of Torksey ware. 6: Cooking pot, Whitby-type ware, Whitby. 7:
Cooking pot, with complex rouletted dec., Chester-type ware, Chester. 8-24: St Neots-type
wares. 8-10: Cooking pots. 8: Berks. 9: St Neots. 10: Cambridge. 11-24: Bowls. 11: Bedford.
12: Cambridge. 13-16, 19-20: Bedford. 17-18, 21: Cambridge. 22-3: Cambs. 24: Seacourt,
Oxford. (Drawings: 1-5: Dunning. 6-7, 9-10, 12, 14, 16-18, 21-3: Hurst. 8, 24: Jope. 11, 13,
15, 19-20: Kennett.)

Fig. 5: ST NEOTS-TYPE WARES.
1-9: Shallow drinking bowls or dishes, Cambs. 10-18: Jugs, 12th c. 10: Leicester. 11: Bedford. 12: With rouletted dec., Oxford. 13: With rouletted dec., Ely. 14-17: Bedford. 18: Developed St Neots-type ware, Leicester. (Drawings: 10, 18: Dunning. 1-9, 11: Hurst. 12: Jope. 13-17: Kennett.)

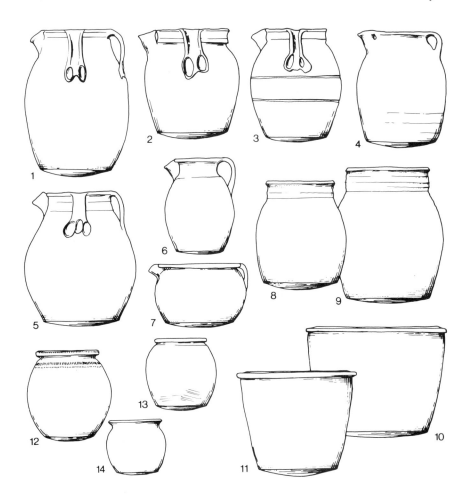

Fig. 6. STAMFORD-TYPE WARES.
1-7: Spouted pitchers, with thin yellow glaze. 1: Leics. 2: Oxford. 3: Stamford. 4: Oxford. 5: Leicester. 6: London. 8-14: Cooking pots or containers, unglazed. 8-11, 14: Leicester. 12: Stamford. 13: Lincs.
(Drawings: 3, 5-6, 8-14: Dunning. 4: Hassall. 2: Jope. 7: Kilmurray. 1: Rudkin.)

Fig. 7. STAMFORD-TYPE WARES AND DEVELOPED STAMFORD WARE.
1-13: Stamford-type ware. 1: Bowl with thumbed strip on rim, Lincs. 2: Cooking pot. 3: Jug, glazed greenish-yellow, Stamford. 4: Bowl, rouletted dec. on rim, Stamford. 9: Lincs. 11: Bowl, rouletted dec. on rim, Lincs. 12: Shallow bowl. 13: Jug, glazed pale green, Leicester. 14-17: Developed Stamford ware, with green glaze. 14: Jug, app. strip dec., Stamford. 15: Bottle, Stamford. 16: Spouted jug, Stamford. 17: Tripod jug, app. strip dec., Stamford. (Drawings: 1, 4-11, 13: Dunning. 3, 15, 17: Hurst. 2, 12, 14, 16: Kilmurray.)

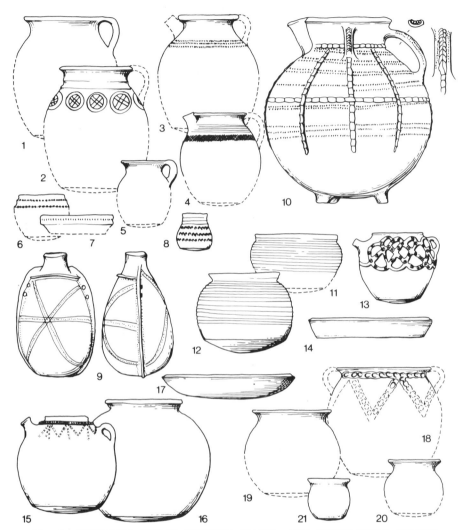

Fig. 8. SOUTHERN WHEEL-THROWN WARES AND WINCHESTER TRIPOD
PITCHER (SAXO-NORMAN).
1-9: Winchester ware. 1: Handled pitcher. 2: Handled jar, with incised roundels. 3-5:
Spouted pitchers. 3, 4: With rouletted dec. 6-7: Bowls. 8: Cup, with dec. of app. scales. 9:
Bottle or costrel, with incised dec. and suspension holes. 10: Spouted tripod pitcher, with
thumbed strips, rouletted dec. and yellow glaze, c. 1100. 11-14: Portchester ware. 11-12:
Cooking pots with external rilling. 13: Spouted pitcher, glazed green, with app. stamped dec.
14: Bowl. 15-17: Michelmersh ware. 15: Spouted pitcher, with stamped dec. 16: Cooking pot.
17: Bowl. 18-21: Exeter ware. 18: Jar, with app. thumbed dec. 19-21: Cooking pots.
(Drawings: 1-2, 4-9: Biddle/Barclay. 10: Biddle. 3, 11-14: Cunliffe. 18-21: Dunning. 15-17:
Hurst.)

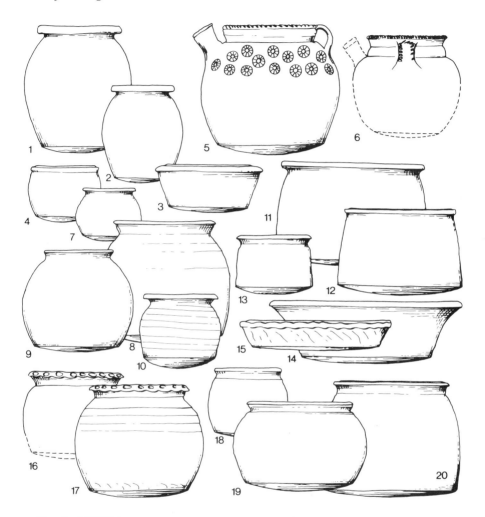

Fig. 9. OXFORD REGION, ELEVENTH- AND TWELFTH-CENTURY COARSE WARES.
1-4: St Neots-type wares. 1-2, 4: Oxford. 3: Yarnton. 5-6: Spouted pitchers, Oxford. 5: With stamped dec. 7-20: Cooking pots or bowls. 7-8: Late 11th to early 12th c., Oxford. 9: Early 12th c., Ascot Doilly. 10-13: Late 11th to early 12th c. 10-11, 13: Oxford. 12: Ascot Doilly. 14-15: Bowls, late 12th c., Oxford. 16: 11th c., Oxford. 17: Late 12th c., Oxford. 18-20: 12th c., Ascot Doilly. (Drawings: 11: Hinton, 1-10, 12-20: Jope.)

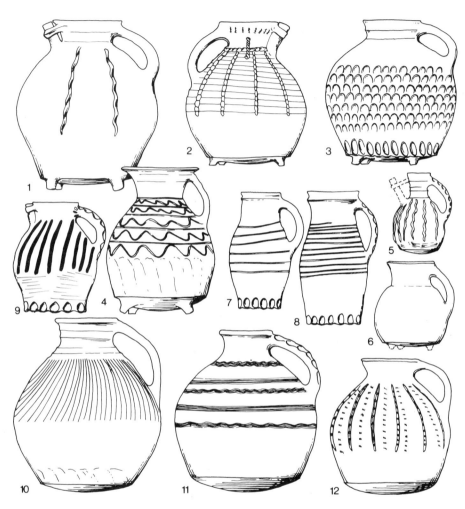

Fig. 10. OXFORD REGION, TWELFTH-CENTURY TRIPOD PITCHERS AND JUGS.
1-4: Tripod pitchers, Oxford. 1-2: With spouts, app. strips and yellow glaze. 3: With
thumbed impressions and green glaze, late 12th to early 13th c. 4: With incised dec. and
yellow glaze. 5: Bottle, with tubular spout, dec. as 1, Oxford. 6: Tripod jug, unglazed shelly
ware, Oxford. 7-8: Jugs with incised spiral lines and yellow glaze, Oxford. 9: Spouted jug,
with app. strips, late 12th to early 13th c., Oxford. 10-12: Unglazed jugs. 10: With burnished
dec., Ascot Doilly. 11: Shelly, with incised lines, Oxford. 12: With app. strips and combed
dec., Ascot Doilly. (Drawings: 1-2, 4, 6, 10, 12: Jope. 3, 5, 7-9, 11: Author, source — Ashmolean Museum.)

Fig. 11. OXFORD REGION, THIRTEENTH-CENTURY WARES.
1: Cistern, with combed dec., Oxford. 2-3: Cooking pots, with thumbed dec. 4: Beehive base, Ascot Doilly. 5-7: Bowl, jug and skillet, from Ascot Doilly kiln, late 12th to early 13th c. 8: Cooking pot, Ascot Doilly. 9: Bowl, with incised dec., Berks. 10: Handled bowl, with thumbed app. strip, Berks.(Drawings: 1: Hinton. 4-10: Jope. 2-3: Sturdy.)

Fig. 12. OXFORD, THIRTEENTH-CENTURY JUGS.
1: With thin glaze. 2: With painted brown stripes. 3: With trailed white slip under yellow glaze. 4: With painted white slip. 5-7: With painted brown slip. 8: With yellow glaze. 9: With trailed red slip, late 13th c. 10: With rouletted app. strips, late 13th c. 11: With app. buff and red strips, late 13th c. 12: With tubular spout, and incised dec. and green glaze. (Drawings: 1-12: Author, source — Ashmolean Museum.)

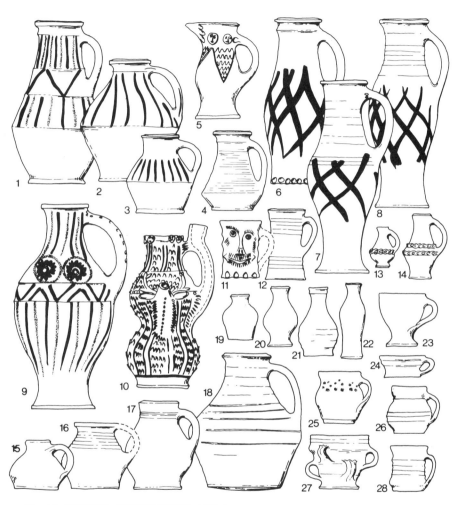

Fig. 13. OXFORD, FOURTEENTH- AND FIFTEENTH-CENTURY VESSELS.
1-4: Carinated jugs. 1-3: With app. strips of alternating buff and red slip (1) or only red slip
(2, 3). 5: Jug, with incised dec. and app. face masks. 6-8: Baluster jugs, with painted red slip
dec. 9: Jug, with buff and red slip and flower motif in roundel. 10: Puzzle-jug, glazed green,
with app. scales, red strips, face masks and deer head over spout. 11-12: Mugs, glazed green,
14th c. 11: With face mask. 13-14: Cruets. 15-18: Jugs, glazed green, 14th to 15th c. 19-22:
Bottles, 15th c. 23-8: Mugs, 15th c. 23-4: Glazed green. 25-8: Copies of Cistercian-type ware
mugs, with red fabric and khaki glaze, 25 with white slip dots.
(Drawings: 1-28: Author, source — Ashmolean Museum.)

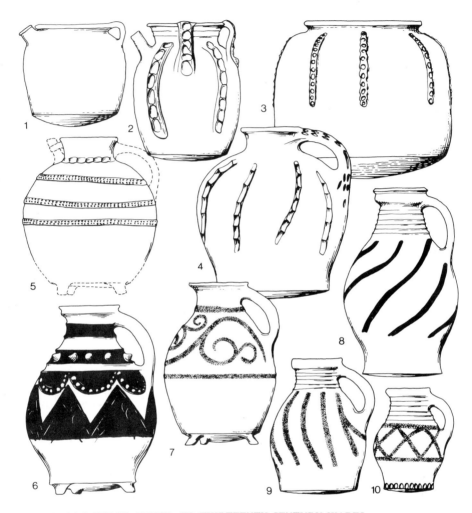

Fig. 14. LONDON, TENTH- TO THIRTEENTH-CENTURY WARES.
1-2: Spouted pitchers, 10th to 11th c. 3-4: Cooking pot and jug, unglazed, of Elstree-type
ware. 3: Northolt. 5-7: Tripod pitchers. 5: With yellow glaze and app. rouletted strips. 6:
With dec. of incised lines, red painted slip and app. pellets. 7: With dec. of white trailed slip.
8-10: Bulbous jugs. 8, 10: With painted brown slip. 9: With painted white slip. (Drawings: 1-
2: Dunning. 3: Hurst. 4-10: Author, sources — 4-5, 8-10, Museum of London; 6, British
Museum; 7, Bank of England Museum.)

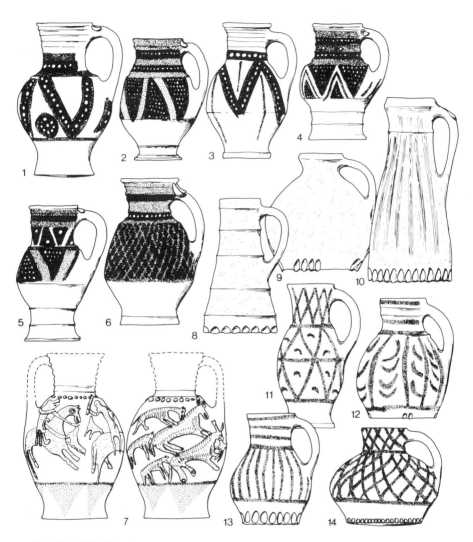

Fig. 15. LONDON, THIRTEENTH-CENTURY JUGS.
1-6: Copies of Rouen jugs, with red fabric, dec. of painted brown slip under trailed white slip lines and dots. 7: Jug with hunting scene in white slip — men on horseback, hounds and stags. 8-10: Jugs of West Kent-type ware, red fabric, white slip and green glaze. 11-14: Jugs, with red fabric and painted white slip dec. (Drawings: 1-14: Author, sources — 1-3, Maidstone Museum; 4, Fitzwilliam Museum, Cambridge; 7, British Museum; 5-6, 8-14, Museum of London.)

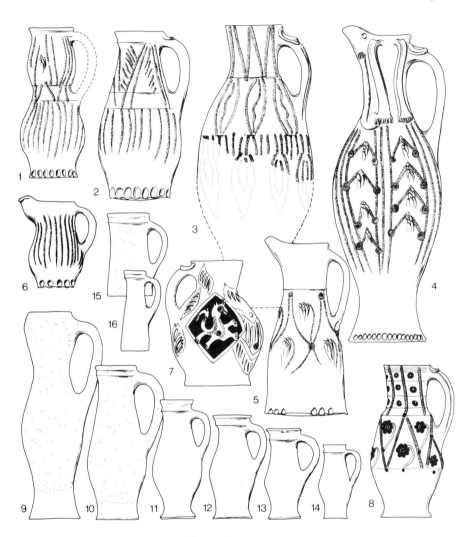

Fig. 16. LONDON, FOURTEENTH-CENTURY JUGS.
1-8: Surrey white ware jugs. 1-6: With dec. of trailed white slip lines. 4-5: Also with dec. of app. impressed pads and scales in white slip. 4: With extra handles at side (restored). 6: With 'parrot-beak' spout. 7: With zoomorphic dec. on brown slip background, and trailed white slip painted green. 8: Copying Rouen shape, floral motifs and trailed slip lines painted green. 9-16: Jugs in red sandy ware, with or without slip or glaze. 9: 'London baluster' type. (Drawings: 1-16: Author, sources — 1-4, 6, 8-16, Museum of London; 5, Bank of England Museum; 7, British Museum.)

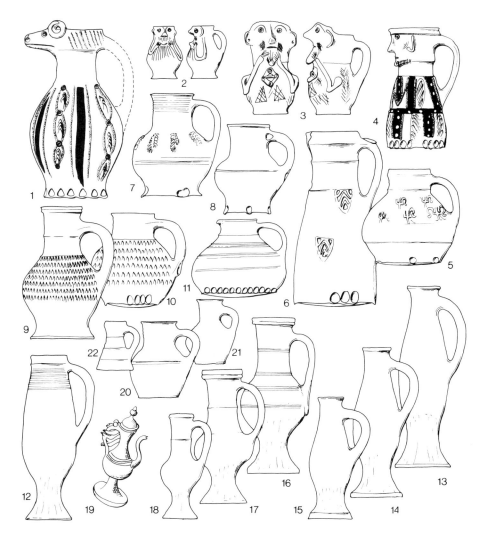

Fig. 17. LONDON, SURREY WHITE WARES, FOURTEENTH-CENTURY AND FIFTEENTH-CENTURY JUGS.
1: Ram's head jug, early 14th c., dec. of trailed lines and scales, and red slip. 2-4: 'Face-on-front' jugs, 14th c. 2-3: With incised dec. 4: With red painted slip, trailed lines painted green, and dots. 5-7: Jugs with impressed fleur-de-lys, shields or wheat-ears, late 14th to early 15th c. 8: Undec. jug, similar to 7. 9-10: Jugs dec. with app. scales, 14th c. 11: Jug, undec., 14th c. 12-18: Baluster jugs similar to products of Kingston kiln, late 14th to early 15th c. 16-18: With shapes influenced by bronze vessels, as in 19, from painting of 1437. 20-2: Jugs, early 15th c. (Drawings: 1-22: Author, sources — 1, 3-5, 7-13, 15-22, Museum of London; 2, British Museum; 6, Victoria and Albert Museum; 14, Fitzwilliam Museum, Cambridge.)

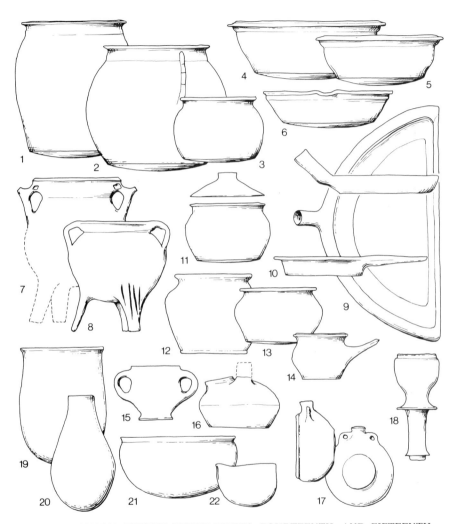

Fig. 18. LONDON, SURREY WHITE WARES, FOURTEENTH- AND FIFTEENTH-CENTURY VESSELS.
1-3: Cooking pots, early 14th c. 4-6: Bowls, glazed green on interior, early 14th c. 7-8: Tripod skillets, 14th c. 9: Meat dish, 14th c. 10: Handled dish, 15th c. 11: Cooking pot with lid, 14th c. 12-13: Cooking pots, 14th to 15th c. 14: Skillet. 15: Cup, glazed green, early 15th c. 16: Urinal, glazed green, 14th to 15th c. 17: Costrel, glazed green, 15th c. 18: Torch, partially glazed green, 15th c. 19-20: Crucible and retort, unglazed, 14th c. 21-2: Crucibles, unglazed, 15th c. (Drawings: 1-22: Author, sources — 1-10, 12-22, Museum of London; 11, Maidstone Museum.)

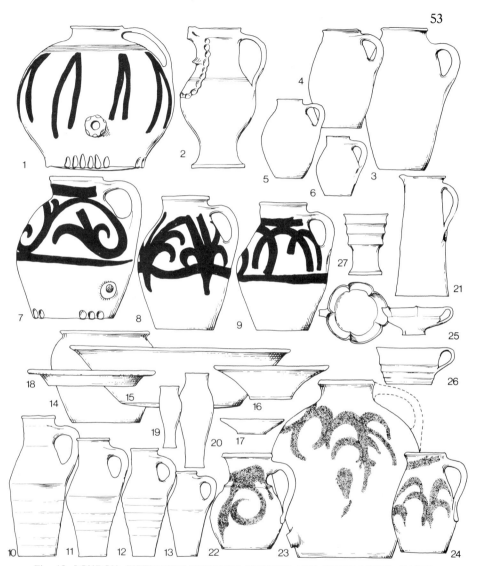

Fig. 19. LONDON, FIFTEENTH-CENTURY VESSELS AND CHEAM KILN GROUP.
1: Bung-hole pitcher, glazed green, with painted red slip stripes. 2: Face jug, green glazed. 3-
6: Jugs similar to products of Cheam kiln. 7-20: Products of Cheam kiln, mid 15th c. 7-9:
Bung-hole pitcher and jugs dec. with painted red slip (9 excavated in London). 10-13:
Biconical jugs. 14: Cooking pot. 15-18: Bowls. 19-20: Bottles. 21: Conical jug, unglazed. 22-
4: Jugs and bung-hole pitcher, mid to late 15th c., with dec. of painted white slip. 25-7: Cups
in Tudor green ware, with green glaze. (Drawings: 1-27: Author, sources — 1, 13, 16,
Guildford Museum; 2-5, 9, 22-4, 26-7, Museum of London; 6-8, Victoria and Albert
Museum; 10-12, 17-19, 21, British Museum; 15, Kingston Museum.)

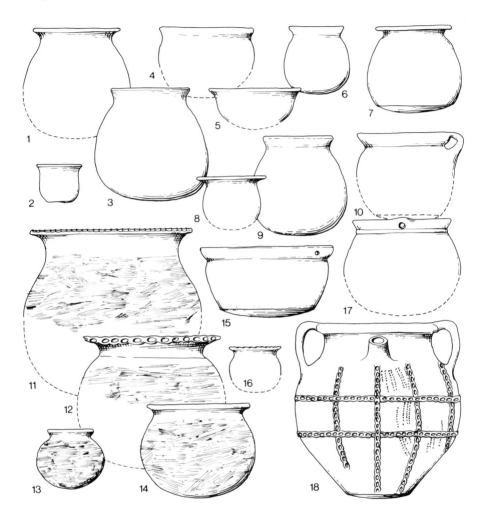

Fig. 20. SOUTHAMPTON, TENTH- TO THIRTEENTH-CENTURY VESSELS.
1-10: Cooking pots and bowls, flint-gritted fabric. 1-6: 10th c. 7-10: 11th to 12th c. 11-14: Scratch-marked ware, 12th c. 15-17: Cooking pots and bowl, 12th c. 18: Spouted pitcher, with dec. of applied thumbed strips, rouletted lines and thin amber-green glaze, 11th c. (Drawings. 1-18: Platt/Coleman-Smith.)

Fig. 21. SOUTHAMPTON, THIRTEENTH- TO FIFTEENTH-CENTURY WARES.
1-7: Cooking pots and bowl, sandy flint-gritted fabric, 13th c. 2-5: Early 13th c. 1, 6, 7: Late
13th c. 8: Skillet, late 13th c. 9: Alembic, early 13th c. 10: Jug, with amber-green glaze, early
13th c. 11: ?Tripod pitcher, with amber glaze, early 13th c. 12-13: Jugs, West Sussex ware,
late 13th c. 14-16: Jugs, early 14th c. 17: Tripod cooking pot, early 14th c. 18-20: Bowls, with
green glaze, 14th c. (Drawings: 1-20: Platt/Coleman-Smith.)

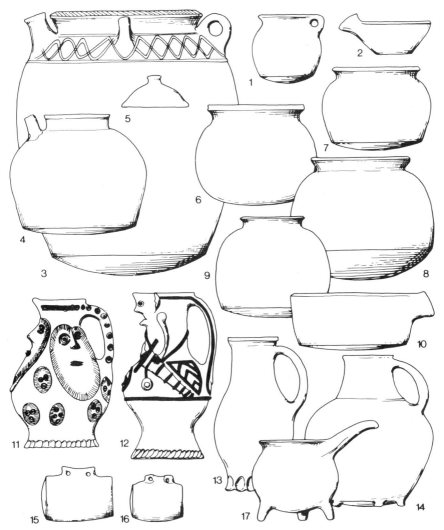

Fig. 22. WINCHESTER AND PORTCHESTER, TENTH- TO FIFTEENTH-CENTURY WARES.
All except 8 from Winchester. 1: Handled cooking pot, flint-gritted fabric, 10th c. 2: Handled bowl, 10th c. 3-4: Spouted pitchers, 11th c. 5: Lid, 11th c. 6-9: Cooking pots, 11th c. 8: From Portchester. 10: Handled bowl, 11th c. 11-12: Anthropomorphic jugs. 11: With stamped pads and eyes of face mask in red clay. 12: With figure holding sword, dec. with red clay. 13-14: Undec. jugs, 13th c. 15-16: Costrels, late 15th c. 17: Tripod skillet, with internal green glaze, 15th c. (Drawings: 1-2, 4-10, 13-14, 17: Cunliffe. 3, 15-16: Dunning. 11-12: Author, source — Winchester City Museum.)

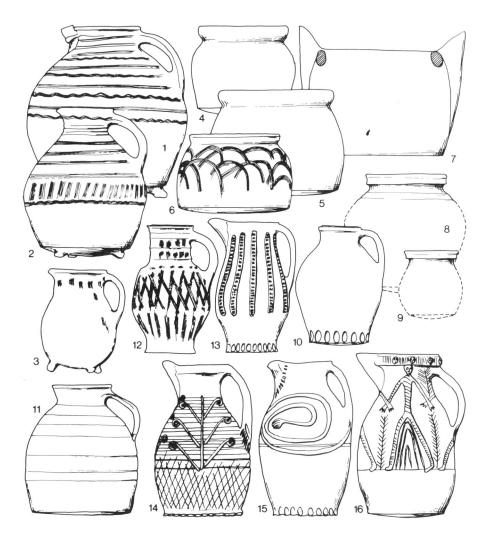

Fig. 23. WEST OF ENGLAND, TENTH- TO FOURTEENTH-CENTURY WARES.
1-3: Tripod pitchers, dec. with incised lines. 1-2: 13th c., Gloucester. 3: *c.* 1100, Corfe. 4-6:
Cooking pots, 12th c., Devon. 4: Exeter. 5: Beere. 6: Dec. with incised lines, Exeter. 7: Bar-
lug cooking pot, St Ives, Cornwall, 9th to 11th c. 8-9: Cooking pots of NW French type, 11th
c., Castle Neroche, Somerset. 10-11: Jugs, early 13th c., Beere. 12-13: Dec. jugs copying
French forms, late 13th c., Exeter. 14-16: Dec. jugs of Ham Green ware, late 13th c. 14, 16:
From Ham Green kilns. 15: Gloucester. (Drawings: 6, 12-13: Allan. 1-2, 7, 15: Dunning. 4-5,
10-11: Jope. 14, 16: Author, source — Bristol City Museum.)

Fig. 24. SOUTH OF ENGLAND, RYE AND LAVERSTOCK KILNS.
1-15: Rye kiln products, late 13th-early 14th c. 1: Jug with stamped pellets. 2-5: Jugs with red painted dec. 6-7: Jugs copying SW French forms, with 'parrot-beak' spouts. 8: Tripod skillet. 9-11: Handled bowls. 12-15: Designs scratched on jugs. 16-22: Laverstock kiln products, late 13th to early 14th c. 16: Bulbous jug. 17-20: Jugs with red painted dec. 18-20: Also with applied stamped pads. 21: Small jug. 22: Skillet. (Drawings: 1-15: Dunning. 16-22: Musty.)

Fig. 25. SOUTH MIDLANDS AND CAMBRIDGE, THIRTEENTH- TO FIFTEENTH-CENTURY WARES.
1-3: Jugs with app. dec., late 13th c., Leicester. 4-6: Cooking pots, 13th c., Leicester. 7: Tripod cauldron, 13th c., Leicester. 8-9: Dec. jugs, late 13th c., Coventry. 8: With anthropomorphic dec. of app. strips, incised lines and three handles. 9: With app. spout, app. strips and pads. 10: Jug, dec. with painted white slip, 13th c., Cambridge. 11-12: Jugs with white slip aprons and incised dec., 15th c., Cambridge (12 found in Canterbury). (Drawings: 11: Addyman/Biddle. 1-9, 12: Dunning. 10: Author, source — Ashmolean Museum.)

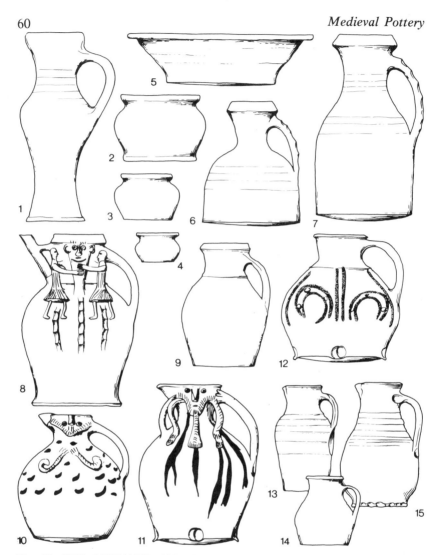

Fig. 26. THE MIDLANDS AND EASTERN ENGLAND, FOURTEENTH AND
FIFTEENTH CENTURIES
1-4: Jug and cooking pots, early 14th c., Nottingham. 5-7: Bowl and jugs, Glasshouse Street
kiln, Nottingham. 8: Green-glazed anthropomorphic jug with spout, beard handles, free-
standing figures, early 14th c., Nottingham. 9: Jug of Nottingham-type fabric, mid 13th c.,
Lincoln. 10-11: Anthropomorphic jugs of Grimston ware, with red painted stripes, 14th c.
10: Cambridge. 11: With extra 'arm' handles, found in Norway. 12: Jug of Toynton All
Saints ware, found in Norway. 13-15: Jugs of Midland purple ware, Leicester. (Drawings: 9:
Adams. 1-7: Alvey. 8, 10-15: Dunning.)

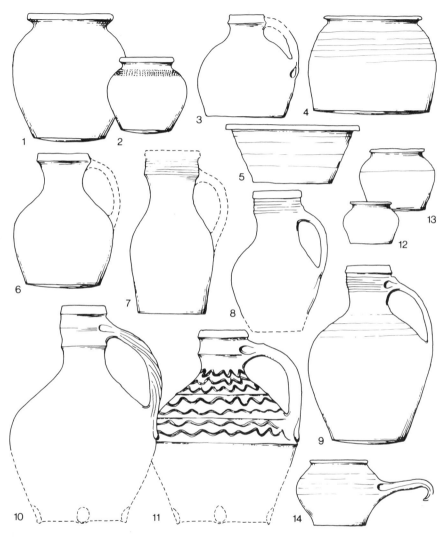

Fig. 27. LINCOLN, TWELFTH TO FOURTEENTH CENTURIES.
1-2: Cooking pots of Saxo-Norman type, shelly fabric, 12th c. 2: With rouletting. 3-4: Jug and cooking pot, shelly ware, 13th to 14th c. 5-6: Bowl and jug, splashed glaze ware. 7-11: Jugs, green-glazed Lincoln ware, late 13th to early 14th c. 10: With 'twisted rope' handle. 11: With incised dec. 12-13: Cooking pots, Lincoln ware, 13th c. 14: Skillet, early 14th c. (Drawings: 3-9, 12-13: Adams. 1-2, 10-11, 14: Coppack.)

Fig. 28. YORK AND YORKSHIRE, TWELFTH TO FOURTEENTH CENTURIES.
1-2: Cooking pots, 12th c., York. 3-6: Jugs of York type. 3-4: With brown painted dec. 3:
Lincoln. 4: York. 5: Dec. with rouletted lines, York. 6: York. 7-9: Jugs from Winksley kiln.
7, 9: With rouletted dec. 8: With tubular spout. 10-12: Tubular-spouted jugs of Scarborough
ware. 10: With 'twisted rope' handle, Scarborough. 11: 'Knight' jug with free-standing
knights on horseback, stag on front, Dartford, Kent. 12: With red painted app. dec.,
Staxton. (Drawings: 12: Brewster. 11: Dunning. 1-9: Le Patourel. 10: Rutter.)

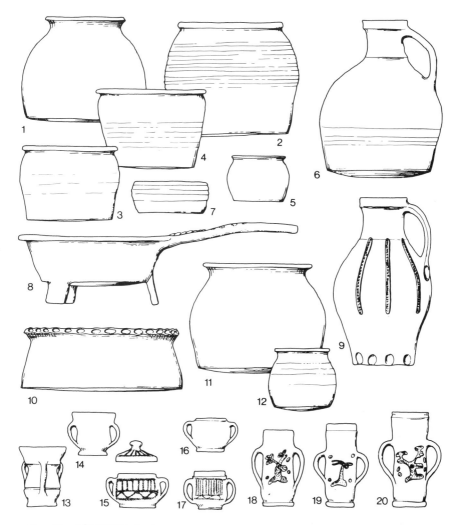

Fig. 29. YORKSHIRE, THIRTEENTH- AND FOURTEENTH-CENTURY AND CISTERCIAN-TYPE WARES.
1-9: Products of Upper Heaton kiln, 13th c. 1-6: Cooking pots. 7: 'Cheese press'. 8: Dec. tripod skillet, with thin green glaze, copying metal prototype. 9: Jug, with app. dec. 10-12: Cooking pots, Staxton. 13-20: Cistercian-type wares. 13-14: Mugs. 15-17: Posset pots. 15, 17: With dec. of trailed white slip. 18-20: Tall mugs, with dec. of stags' heads in trailed white slip. 14, 17, 19-20: York. 15, 18: Potovens kiln. 13: Silcoates kiln. (Drawings: 13-16, 18-19: Brears. 10-12: Brewster. 1-9: Manby. 17, 20: Le Patourel.)

Index